PEG COUCH

creating

SMUDGE STICKS

15 Projects to Remove Negative Energy
and Promote Wellness

REDFeather™
MIND | BODY | SPIRIT

4880 Lower Valley Road, Atglen, PA 19310

Designed by Brenda McCallum
Cover design by Danielle Farmer
Type set in Adorne Pomander/Gotham Light

Project photography by Mike Couch
Cover and Make Your First Bundle photography by Bob Smith
Meet the Maker photography by Jordan Pay (www.jordanpay.com)
Project introductions and intentions by Mary Kate Murray

ISBN: 978-0-7643-5999-6
Printed in India

Published by Red Feather Mind, Body, Spirit
An imprint of Schiffer Publishing, Ltd.
4880 Lower Valley Road
Atglen, PA 19310
Phone: (610) 593-1777; Fax: (610) 593-2002
E-mail: Info@schifferbooks.com
Web: www.redfeathermbs.com

For our complete selection of fine books on this and related subjects, please visit our website at www.schifferbooks.com. You may also write for a free catalog.

Schiffer Publishing's titles are available at special discounts for bulk purchases for sales promotions or premiums. Special editions, including personalized covers, corporate imprints, and excerpts, can be created in large quantities for special needs. For more information, contact the publisher.

The following images are courtesy of Shutterstock.com.

Herbal tea ingredients on a white background © Darina Saukh. Dried flowers in bottles with twinkle lights © CoralAntlerCreative. Hipster couple embracing in windy field © Bogdan Sonjachnyj. Woman with headdress made of feathers and flowers © Antonyshyn Anna. White rose © worapan kong. Star anise, cinnamon sticks, cloves and pepper © Olena Ukhova. Rose-hips © Valentyn Volkov. Small bouquet of flowers © Natalia Greeske. Top view of bath tub with flower petals and lemon slices © Alena Ozerova. Bouquet of fresh lavender flowers © TanaCh. Summer wreath of garden flowers © lesyaskripak. Handmade soap and lavender on bamboo background © PLen. Body scrub of sea salt with lemon © Julia Sudnitskaya. Smudge kit for spiritual practices with natural elements © Pinkasevich. Woman wearing warm woolen sweater and fashion jewellery © Alena Ozerova. Sage candle with amethyst and twinkle lights © CoralAntlerCreative. Grey silver leaves © JONG 16899. Marigold © Julia Sudnitskaya.

SAFETY DISCLAIMER

Not recommended for internal use.

Never leave burning unattended.

We recommend that you consult with a qualified healthcare practitioner before using herbal products, particularly if you are pregnant, are nursing, have allergies, or are on any medications.

For educational purposes only. This information has not been evaluated by the Food and Drug Administration. It is not intended to diagnose, treat, cure, or prevent any disease.

Acknowledgments

This book was a true collaboration and would not have been possible without the help, guidance, and support of many people to whom I am grateful. Thank you to my husband, Michael, who doubled as a photographer on this project. To my son, Sam, who's creative mind is a constant source of inspiration. To Mary Kate Murray for her work on the project introductions and intentions. And, to Karen Heltzel for her assistance on the meanings and symbolism of plants, flowers, and herbs. I would also like thank Johanna Pay for sharing her story and photographs of her work in this book. And finally, my thanks and gratitude to the team at Schiffer Publishing for their trust, collaboration, and guidance on this project.

Contents

PROJECTS

Preface

Smudging, the act of burning sacred herbs for protection and to cleanse negative energy, is an ancient practice, deeply rooted in Native American tradition but also used in cultures around the world. How does it work? Research has shown that when the leaves of sage and other herbs are burned, the smoke acts as a purifier to remove negative ions from the air—thus cleansing not only the physical space but also mind and body of the user. Smudging can be used in many situations, such as when moving into a new living space (to clear it of stagnant or negative energies), after conflict (to cleanse yourself of any negativity left behind), or as a part of your daily meditation practice (to center and focus).

Smudging is traditionally done with white sage, which is a sacred plant and native to California and Mexico. However, white sage is currently on a watch list for species at risk, and there is much controversy over the harvesting of it for commercial use. For that reason, we have approached this book from the position of using what is local to you and what can sustainably be harvested. We highly encourage that you use herbs and flowers from your own garden or purchase them from a reputable farm or supplier.

The perspective of this book is on creativity (as seen through the use of various flowers and other nontraditional ingredients), personalization, and the positive potential of intention. We suggest fifteen recipes, each with specific meanings associated with the ingredients used, but the hope is that you will embrace this practice and make it personal to your own interests and experiences. Always remember to use what is local and sustainable, and what you are drawn to personally.

A final note: Because we are making these smudge sticks from fresh ingredients, they will look different than the premade bundles you have seen, or have used before. After making each bundle, you will need to hang it in a cool, dry place for four to six weeks. Once it is dry, you can burn your bundle and experience the positive benefits. Throughout the drying process, your bundle will take on a different look—appreciate all phases. It's amazing to see your bundle transform, and wonderful to extend the life of your plants/herbs long after their peak growth time.

We honor the rich heritage of smudging as we embrace this practice and make it personal to ourselves and our daily lives.

DISCLAMER: Always be sure to remove any decorative elements prior to burning to ensure safety and best results.

The perspective of this book is on creativity...
personalization, and positive potential of intention.

Welcome

Whether you are new to making your own smudge sticks or have an established practice of making and using them, I am grateful that you've found this book. I hope that it will inspire you to get out into nature, look at herbs and flowers in a new way, harvest them sustainably, and bring them into your home, where you will lovingly arrange and shape them into a variety of bundles. As your bundles are dried and ready for burning, it's my hope that you will be inspired by the suggested mediations that go along with each project, and experience the benefit of this sacred tradition.

May a sense of calm and peace wash over you. May you be filled with light and love. And may you radiate what is inside you to the world outside.

Let's get started!

Peg

Essential Ingredients
TO CHOOSE FOR YOUR PROJECTS

Herbs, Flowers, Greens, and More

HERBS AND GREENS

Bay laurel

Cedar

Dusty miller

Hosta

Eucalyptus, silver dollar

Eucalyptus, baby blue

Juniper

Lavender

Palo santo (of the plant kingdom)

Rosemary

Sage, common

Sage, White

Sweetgrass

FLOWERS

Baby's breath

Carnation, pink (dark)

Carnation, pink (light)

Carnation, yellow

Dahlia (red)

Delphinium

Rose, white

Rose, light pink

Rose, pink

Rose, red

Wildflowers, various colors as desired

Marigold

Statice (purple)

Thistle

Yarrow

ADDITIONAL ITEMS

Abalone shell or bowl

Candle

Corn husk

Crystals (amethyst, selenite)

Feather

Matches

Twine (organic, natural dye, various colors and weights)

Toothpick

Garden scissors

Rubber bands

Love letter or scrapbook paper

Tape

Petal Play

Creative Exploration with Plants, Herbs, and Flowers

Creating smudge sticks is a sensory experience. I encourage you to play with your stems, flowers, and petals prior to making your sticks. At first, it may feel unnatural to pick off petals and cut beautiful flower heads from their stems, but this exercise will help you get used to petal play!

Arrange your natural materials into beautiful shapes, or try making mandalas from their petals. Always remember that this exercise and making smudge sticks are not about perfection. Feel the texture of each individual element and appreciate it. Inhale the aromas and let the beauty of nature inspire, relax, and calm you as you prepare for making.

"Study nature, love nature, stay close to nature. It will never fail you."

Frank Lloyd Wright

Make Your First Bundle

Step-by-Step Instructions

1. GATHER BASE MATERIALS

Pick up the first stem of your base material and position it on your hand. Layer each additional stem, one on top of the other, so that they form a balanced bundle.

2. LAYER SECONDARY MATERIALS

Layer the stems of any additional herbs or flowers that you wish to include in your bundle on top of your base.

3. WRAP

Cut a piece of twine approximately three times the length of your bundle. Tie a knot with the twine at the base of your bundle, securing on the backside.

Gently wrap your bundle with twine, moving in an upward fashion, diagonally. When you reach the top, continue wrapping downward diagonally, crisscrossing each layer as you go.

Secure a knot at the base of the twine, leaving enough room to create a loop (that you will use to hang your bundle to dry).

Trim the base so all stems are blunt, and snip any loose or ill-positioned leaves or petals (manicure to your taste).

4. DRY

Hang your bundle in a cool, dry location for four to six weeks or until it is completely dry. Note that your bundle will shrink upon drying, so you may wish to retie or adjust any loose strings before using.

In this book, we will be making many bouquet-style smudges—meaning the tops are left open, which makes for a lovely design. For the purpose of functionality (or style preference), you may wish to continue wrapping your bundles all the way to the top before wrapping downward. This is totally fine. Always remember that this is a personal pursuit . . . do what works best for you, and always keep safety in mind!

"Let us fill our hearts with our own compassion-toward ourselves and towards all living beings."

Thich Nhat Hanh

How to Burn

Step-by-Step Instructions

1. PREPARE

Gather an abalone shell or heatproof bowl, matches, and smudge. Open windows so that the negative energy can flow outside. Set your intention.

2. LIGHT

Hold the flame against the end of your smudge stick until it catches fire evenly. Then, gently blow on the end to extinguish the flame. At this point, your smudge stick should be producing a plume of smoke. There should never be an open flame on your stick that could catch something on fire.

3. SMUDGE

Walk around the space you wish to smudge, holding the stick in one hand over your shell or bowl in the other (so that it catches any ashes that may fall).

Recite your intention as you travel throughout your space. Be sure to smudge in all corners where stagnant or negative energy can collect.

Smudge your body by slowly moving the stick around yourself, being cautious not to let it come into contact with your body. It is common to use a feather to help move the smoke through the air.

4. EXTINGUISH

When complete, extinguish your smudge into the shell or bowl so that the smoldering is out. Leave your smudge stick in this bowl until it is complexly cooled or until using again.

SAFE SMUDGING: Never leave a lit smudge stick unattended around flammable objects, children, or pets.

Meet the Maker

Johanna Pay

Elements of Sage

I started burning sage when I lived in the city about five years ago. I burned sage in our rental home to cleanse the space of stagnant and negative energy. It was important to me, to cleanse and bless our home so that my family and I would not be affected by lingering energy from previous tenants. When I first started smudging, I noticed swift, positive changes in the energy of our home and life. My sage-burning mantra consisted of "casting out old, negative vibrations"

and calling in blessings of "peace, love and prosperity." The sage-burning ritual helps me to connect with the universe. With meditation and sage-burning, I could feel a shift toward positive energy. This beautiful holistic practice brought a peaceful, loving and productive vibe into our home and lives. So many blessings and opportunities started manifesting. It was as though the universe had heard my intentions loud and clear.

The power of your intention and vibration into the universe should never be underestimated. The sage-burning ritual has taught me to always strive to be my highest self and to allow myself to dream the happiest life filled with purpose and excitement. I started Elements of Sage in the summer of 2018. It is my wish to collectively raise the vibration of this Earth. What better way than to incorporate these beautiful healing herbs into our lives? Mountain sagebrush, juniper, cedar, lavender, mint, and roses all possess a powerful and beautiful natural energy. This energy can be used to uplift your space, to cleanse your aura, and to create a life with a higher vibrational energy.

In our modern-day world, our homes and spaces get a build-up of stagnant energy, from expressions of pain, sadness, and stress to many other feelings. This build-up of negative energy can have an effect on our moods causing irritability, low productivity levels, trouble focusing, and overall low energy. It is important to keep in mind that the energy in your home should be cleansed as often as you physically clean your home. By maintaining a regular energy cleansing in your home when using a sage, herb, or flower-burning ritual, you can harness a positive flow of energy. This positive energy can have a direct effect on your well-being. With this positive energy in your space, you will feel more energy, focus, mental-clarity, and you will even sleep better.

Sage smoke has antibacterial properties and is known to decrease airborne viruses and bacteria in the home. Next time someone has been sick in your home, remember to get your sage bundle and cleanse the space to keep the airborne bacteria clean. The smoke from dried sage and healing herbs changes the ionic composition of the air by converting positive ions into negative ions. Negative ions come from the natural world such as forests, beaches, gardens, and waterfalls. When we go into nature, we naturally feel uplifted, more clear, and fresh. By bringing the natural elements of sage smoke into your space, you create these same vibrations and input negative ions from nature, into your home and space. The idea is to invite wonderful high vibes from the natural world into your home.

Each healing herb has its own unique healing qualities. Sage, juniper, and cedar are all excellent for cleansing, protection, and purging negativity,. Mint is uplifting and cleanses and blesses your space with positivity. Lavender is tranquil, calming, and peaceful. Rose invites love, happiness, and creativity. By blending these herbs together in a sage bundle, you can cleanse and bless your space with a sage-burning ritual. Purification through sage smoke can be used for so many occasions in life, such as moving into a new home, job transitions, healing, energy work, losing a loved one, moon magic, creating a productive workspace, meditating, working on relationships, and so much more.

At Elements of Sage, each of our bundles is charged with a healing crystal and dedicated to a specific healing purpose. The crystals add even more healing properties and can amplify your healing and intentions as you burn sage.

For more healing-benefit details about sage bundles, please visit our website: www.elementsofsage.com.

Courageous-Heart Smudge
with White Sage, Dried Lavender & Yarrow

Start over, my darling. Be brave enough to find the life you want and courageous enough to chase it. Then start over, and love yourself the way you were always meant to.

Madalyn Beck

How strength and courage show up will be different for different people at different times. What can we do that will help build our resilience and support ourselves in knowing our innate ability to act from strength and courage?

SUGGESTED INTENTION:
As I burn this smudge, may it help me to draw upon my inner resources. May I know myself as calm, yet strong. May I know myself as courageous. May I honor the big ways that I show up bravely, and may I also see the everyday ways that I demonstrate strength and courage.

INGREDIENTS

- White sage, 1 small bundle (dried)—purification
- Lavender, 17 stems (dried)—serenity, calm
- Yarrow, 1 stem (dried)— strength
- Rubber band (1)
- Twine (white or purple)

1 GATHER YOUR MATERIALS

You will need a bundle of dried white sage (prepurchased or previously made), dried lavender, and dried yarrow.

2. POSITION LAVENDER AND SNIP TO SIZE

Position the lavender on the sage bundle so that the base of the flowers is level with the top of the sage. Snip the lavender stems so they are blunted with the bottom of the sage.

3. SECURE LAVENDER

Temporarily secure your lavender stems with a small rubber band. This will allow you to more easily work with the materials prior to wrapping with twine.

4. POSITION YARROW

Position the yarrow on top of the lavender so that the yellow flower is level with the top of the sage bundle. Trim any yarrow petals as necessary so that it fits snuggly against the bundle.

6

5. SNIP YARROW TO SIZE

Snip the yarrow stem so that it is blunt with the bottom of the sage bundle. You are now ready to wrap your bundle.

6. SECURE TWINE WITH KNOT

Wrap one layer of twine around the bottom of your bundle, approximately 1" from the bottom. Flip the bundle and secure the twine with a knot on the backside (leaving a long tail of twine).

7. WRAP BUNDLE WITH TWINE

Working with the tail, wrap your twine diagonally up the sage bundle and back down again so that the two layers crisscross. Secure the two ends of twine at the bottom with a knot.

8. FINISHING TOUCH

Remove rubber band from lavender stems. Review your bundle from all angles. Clip any unwanted or ill-positioned petals. Project complete!

Stress Relief Smudge

with Lavender & Sage

You will find that it is necessary to let things go; simply for the reason that they are heavy.

C. JoyBell C.

Stress is all around us. How can we discharge the stress within us to create more balance and peace? The breath is one of the surest ways to calm our sympathetic nervous systems. Just three deep breaths can shift the brain into more regulation.

Suggested Intention:

As I burn this smudge, I breathe in deeply the calming scents and use this breath to calm my brain and body. May I know myself as peaceful, centered, and relaxed.

INGREDIENTS

- Lavender, 6 stems (with flowers)—serenity, calm
- Sage (common), 6 stems—purification
- Twine (purple)

1 GATHER YOUR MATERIALS

You will need fresh sage and flowering lavender. If you prefer a larger bundle, be sure to have additional clippings of each herb available.

2. PREPARE STEMS

Tidy your stems by snipping away any leaves that may be yellowing or growing too low on the stem.

3. GATHER SAGE

Pick up your first stem of sage and position it on your hand. Layer each additional stem, one on top of the other, so that they form a balanced bundle.

4. ADD LAVENDER

Layer each stem of lavender onto your sage bundle, positioned so that the flower heads start just a little lower than the sage. The goal is to be able to see each layer of herb.

5

6

5. SECURE TWINE WITH KNOT

Wrap one layer of twine around bundle at the base of the flower heads. Flip the bundle and secure the twine with a knot on the backside (leaving ample twine on your spool for wrapping).

6. WRAP BUNDLE WITH TWINE

Working with the remaining twine, wrap diagonally down the sage bundle and back up again so that the two layers crisscross. Secure the two ends of twine at the top with a knot.

This bundle is tied from top down. Tip: If stems are varying lengths, begin wrapping at top to secure the shortest lengths first.

7. FINAL TRIM

Review your bundle from all angles. Clip any unwanted or ill-positioned leaves or petals.

8. FINISHING

Your bundle is complete. Remember to hang it upside down in a cool dry place for four to six weeks before burning.

Happy-Heart Smudge
with Sage, Pink & Yellow Carnation & Hosta

Ever since happiness heard your name,
it has been running through the streets trying to find you.

Hafiz

Sometimes the quickest route to happiness is to embrace the fullness of our experience—including our unhappy feelings. Constricting the flow of any feeling constricts the flow of all feelings.

SUGGESTED INTENTION:

As I burn this vibration-raising smudge, I wrap my arms around the fullness of me and beam love at all of it. May this loving acceptance enable the golden light of happiness to seep into my bones, into my heart, and into my mind, until I am filled with its warmth.

INGREDIENTS

- Sage (common), 11 stems—purification
- Hosta, 1 leaf
- Carnation (yellow), 2 flowers—heart healing, happiness
- Carnation (dark pink), 3 flowers—heart healing, love
- Basting twine (natural, thinner weight)
- Twine (green)

1 GATHER YOUR MATERIALS

You will need fresh sage, yellow carnations, bright pink carnations, and a plant leaf; I used hosta but you can substitute with what is available.

2

3

4

5

2. GATHER SAGE

Pick up your first stem of sage, and position it on your hand. Layer each additional stem, one on top of the other, so that they form a balanced bundle.

3. LAYER PINK CARNATION

Position your pink carnations so they are just below the highest sage leaves. I am using three flower heads (one stem).

4. ADD YELLOW CARNATION

Layer your yellow carnations just under the pink carnations. Again, the goal here is to stagger each layer so you have three visible rows.

5. BASTE WITH TWINE

Secure the stems with basting twine, wrapping diagonally up and down. This will secure the stems for the next step.

6. WRAP WITH LEAF

Wrap the plant leaf around your bundle, covering the basting twine. This will give your bundle a nice finished look.

7. WRAP BUNDLE WITH FINISHING TWINE

Wrap twine around the top of the leaf. Flip the bundle and secure a knot in the back. Then, continue wrapping the twine diagonally down the leaf and back up again. Secure in the back with a final knot.

8. FINISHING

Review your bundle from all angles. Clip any unwanted or ill-positioned leaves or flowers at the top. Remember to hang in a cool, dry place for four to six weeks prior to burning.

Pure-Energy Smudge

with Eucalyptus, Statice & White Carnation

Sit quietly and listen for a voice that will say, "Be more silent."
As that happens, your soul starts to revive.

Rumi

Almost every day, our modern lives pull us in multiple directions. Our bodies will always tell us that we are fatigued and need to recharge, but we have become practiced at not listening to them soon enough. How can we notice sooner and then revive ourselves more deeply and fully?

SUGGESTED INTENTION:

As I burn this fragrant smudge, I breathe rejuvenating energy into every cell in my body. I feel the flow of energy, like the waves of the ocean, washing over me, cleansing me, and filling me with positive energy.

INGREDIENTS

- Eucalyptus (baby blue), 3 stems—fresh energy, revival and renewal
- Sage, 12 stems—purification
- Carnation (white, small), 3 flowers—heart healing, purification
- Statice (purple), 6 stems
- Thistle, 2 stems—protection
- Basting twine (white)
- Twine (white or purple)
- Toothpick

1 GATHER YOUR MATERIALS

You will need fresh sage, eucalyptus, white carnations, thistle, and statice. If you prefer a larger bundle, be sure to have additional clippings of each herb available.

2. GATHER SAGE

Organize your sage into two neat and balanced halves. Turn one half upside down and join it to the others so there are leaves at both ends; this will create a balanced bundle with thickness at top and bottom.

3. ADD STATICE

Layer your purple statice on top of the sage; snip the stems so that they are blunt with the sage stems.

4. BASTE WITH TWINE

Use the lighter-weight twine to baste (or temporarily secure) the bundle, and set it aside.

5. CLIP EUCALYPTUS LEAVES

Using your garden scissors, gently snip a set of eucalyptus leaves off the stem. Snip very close to the leaf on the top, and leave as much stem as possible on the bottom.

6. CONTINUE CLIPPING LEAVES

Cut five additional pairs of eucalyptus leaves off the main stem. Set the leaves aside. These will be used for the decorative wrapping later.

7. Layer carnation and thistle

Add thistle to the right and left sides of your bundle. Then add carnations in the center. Secure again with basting twine. Your bundle is now fully assembled with flowers, and we will move on to the decorative wrap.

5

6

7

8. PIERCE BUNDLE

Position a toothpick just below the carnations in the center of the stems. Gently press on the toothpick to pierce a hole straight through the stems. Do not remove the toothpick.

9. INSERT EUCALYPTUS

Pick up one of the clipped eucalyptus leaves and gently insert it into the hole drilled by the toothpick. Wiggle the toothpick as needed to open the hole. Remove toothpick after stem is fully inserted.

10. CONTINUE INSERTING

Insert a second hole with the toothpick just below the first eucalyptus leaf and insert another eucalyptus leaf as you did in the previous step.

11. FINISH ADDING LEAVES

Continue adding eucalyptus leaves until none are remaining. Use your hands to press the leaves back, revealing what the final wrap looks like.

12. WRAP AND COMPLETE

Wrap the finishing twine around the bottom of your bundle and secure a knot in the back. Wrap upward diagonally until you reach the top of the eucalyptus, then wrap your way down the bundle to the bottom, crisscrossing over the first wrap. Remember to hang your bundle in a cool, dry place for four to six weeks before burning.

CREATIVE IDEAS FOR EXTRA MATERIALS

Once you get started making smudge sticks, you will begin to amass a large collection of herbs, flowers, and greenery. Throughout the process of cutting and sizing greens, you will inevitably have extras . . . lots of extras! Don't throw them away; there is so much you can do with them. Give your remaining flower petals, herbs, and greens a second, or third, life!

HOMEMADE HERBAL SOAPS: It's surprising simple to make your own soaps by using melt-and-pour soap bases. Simply dry herbs (lavender is a wonderful choice) and add to your soap base. Let cool in a soap mold of your choice, pop out, and use or gift.

SALT SCRUBS: Combine minced and dried herbs (rosemary is a great choice) with coconut oil, almond oil, granulated white sugar, and the essential oil of your choice to create an invigorating and healthful facial scrub. Small jam jars make great containers to hold your scrub. Add lemon for additional revitalization.

FLOWER BATHS: There is nothing more luxurious for an evening of self-care than a flower bath. Simply pour any remaining flower petals into a warm bath, light a few candles, open a good book, and indulge.

WREATHS: Weave extra herb sprigs around small wreath forms or wire to create a fresh and welcoming accent to your front door. Depending on the herbs you use, this wreath can also add an extra touch of protection and blessing for your home (e.g., rosemary or cedar). Add flowers for a pop of color and beauty.

Love & Light Smudge
with Rosemary & Rose

Love is a light that shines from heart to heart.

John Denver

Putting our energies into best supporting our health, happiness, and well-being is a lifelong goal to return to again and again as our lives ebb and flow. How can we call love and light into our lives?

SUGGESTED INTENTION:

As I burn this beautiful smudge and inhale, I breathe in deeply the love and light all around me. And as I exhale, I breathe out all that does not serve me and all that I am ready to release. May the love and light within me radiate out from me.

INGREDIENTS

- Rosemary, 5 stems/sprigs—strength, protection, memory
- Spray rose (light pink), 2 stems—love, beauty, happiness, blessings
- Spray rose (dark pink), 1 stem—love, beauty, happiness, blessings
- Twine (white)

1 GATHER YOUR MATERIALS

You will need rosemary stalks for your base and both light- and dark-pink roses for color and texture.

2. GATHER ROSEMARY

Pick up your first stem of rosemary and position it on your hand. Layer each additional stem, one on top of the other, so that they form a neat bundle. Place a few stems upside down if it helps to balance your bundle.

3. PREPARE ROSES

Snip individual flowers off the main cluster (two light pink and one dark pink). Note: Spray roses differ from long-stem roses in that they have many flowers growing on a stem versus just one.

4. SNIP STEM

Turn the rose upside down and snip the stem completely off. The goal is to remove as much of the stem without compromising the flower head. This will help the flower lie flat on the bundle.

5

5. CONTINUE SNIPPING STEMS

Repeat the prior step on the remaining two rose heads so that you have all three flowers snipped.

6. PLAN FLOWER PLACEMENT

Place each of the three roses in order (light pink, dark pink, light pink) on the sage bundle. This will help you gauge where to begin tying the twine in the next step.

7. SECURE BUNDLE

Wrap twine around the top of the bundle and secure it with a knot. Do not continue further at this point.

6

7

8. ADD FLOWERS AND WRAP

Add the first light rose to the bundle and secure it. Then, pick up the tail of the twine with your other hand and continue wrapping diagonally, right over the rose. Continue to add flowers and wrap downward until you reach the bottom.

9. COMPLETE WRAPPING

Now wrap in the opposite direction, wrapping upward in a diagonal fashion and crisscrossing the existing wrap. When complete, secure your wrap with a knot in the back of the bundle. Tip: Manipulate flower petals as necessary to ensure that they are tethered "open" with petals to the outside versus "inward" and thus hiding the center of the flower.

10. FINAL TRIM

Review your bundle from all angles. Clip any unwanted or ill-positioned rosemary petals.

11. FINISHING

If necessary, trim each end of the bundle so that they are nice and even. Your bundle is complete! Remember to hang in a cool, dry place for four to six weeks before burning.

Anti-Anxiety Smudge

with Bay Laurel, Rosemary, White Rose & Dahlia

Patience is the way out of anxiety.

Rumi

Anxiety can grip us and wash over us like rising water. It is important that we find ways to ease our worried minds and calm our anxious hearts.

SUGGESTED INTENTION:

As I burn this peace-inducing smudge, I breathe in deeply. I remind myself that I am safe and I am loved. I imagine safe and loving arms wrapping around me and comforting me. I repeat this mantra and breathe in this scent until I feel release in my body, heart, and mind.

INGREDIENTS

- Bay laurel, 3 stems—banishment of negativity, healing
- Rosemary, 4 sprigs—strength, protection, memory
- Spray roses (white, miniature), 6 flowers—love, beauty, happiness, blessings
- Dahlia, red (small)—dreams
- Twine (white)
- Optional: tiger's eye crystal

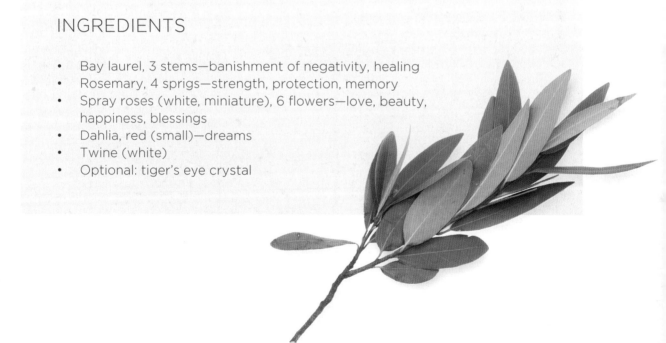

1 GATHER YOUR MATERIALS

You will need laurel for your base, several stalks of
rosemary for texture, spray roses for contrast, and a
deep-red dahlia for a dramatic focal point.

2. GATHER LAUREL

Join two laurel clippings together to form the base of your bundle. Leave the third laurel clipping aside; it will be added in later.

3. LAYER ROSEMARY

Hold the laurel with one hand and layer all but one rosemary stalk on top of it. Fan the rosemary out so that it mirrors the width of the laurel. Keep the remaining rosemary aside.

4. ADD ROSES

Hold the bundle securely with one hand and place the white roses in the center of it, just a little below the rosemary and laurel (so you see all elements).

5. ADD FINAL LAUREL AND DAHLIA

Place your third laurel clipping on top of the bundle; position the leaves so they go around, but do not obstruct, the roses. Place the dahlia in the center of the bundle.

6. ADD ROSEMARY

Layer the final stalk of rosemary onto your bundle. Position it so that it wraps around the dahlia and does not obstruct it.

7. WRAP BUNDLE

Working with the tail, wrap your twine diagonally up the sage bundle and back down again so that the two layers crisscross. Secure the two ends of the twine at the bottom with a knot.

8. FINISHING TOUCH

Review your bundle from all angles. Clip any unwanted or ill-positioned leaves. Remember to hang your bundle in a cool, dry place for four to six weeks before burning.

House-Blessing Smudge
with Cedar, Sage, Carnation & Palo Santo

Coming home is one of the most beautiful things

Andre Rieu

It is said that if we dream about a house, we are dreaming about ourselves. Homes are that meaningful to us. Our homes are the containers of our lives, our loves, our hopes and fears, our feelings, and our needs. We could look at them as simply walls and floors, but our lives imbue them with the specific energies of all who live there.

SUGGESTED INTENTION:

As I burn this smudge, I call in blessings for this home. May energies that support enter, energies that would harm be banished, and the love inside be amplified.

INGREDIENTS

- Palo santo, 1 stick—purification, creativity
- Cedar, 2 stems (18" long)—releasing negativity, cleansing
- Sage, 5 stems—purification
- Carnation (white) 3 flowers—heart healing
- Twine (brown)
- Rubber band

1 GATHER YOUR MATERIALS

You will need cedar for the base, sage for texture, white carnation for contrast, and palo santo for additional cleansing.

2. PREP CEDAR

Using sharp garden scissors, snip individual stems off the cedar bough.

3. SNIP ALL BRANCHES

Continue snipping until you have worked your way through all of the little stems on your bough.

4. GATHER CEDAR

One-by-one, layer the cedar stems onto your hand. The goal is to create an even bundle, so alternate or turn branches upside down as you see fit. Reserve a few cedar stems for later.

5. LAYER SAGE

Hold the cedar bundle in your hand and layer the sage stems one at a time so that they are worked into a neat bundle.

6. ADD CARNATIONS

Position the carnations onto your bundle so that they sit nicely on the sage.

7. FINISH WITH CEDAR

Add the cedar that you had in reserve over the carnation stems. Manipulate the cedar as necessary to ensure that it does not obstruct the carnations.

8. ADJUST YOUR BUNDLE

Because the cedar is slick, it may want to slide on you . . . so now is a good time to make any final adjustments.

9. SECURE TEMPORARILY

Secure your bundle with a small rubber band. This will ensure that your materials stay in place while you move on to the next steps.

10. POSITION PALO SANTO

Layer your palo santo on top of your bundle directly in the center—below the carnations and in the middle of the stems.

11. SECURE TWINE WITH KNOT

Wrap one layer of basting twine around the bottom of your bundle; flip it over and secure the twine with a knot on the backside (leaving a long tail of twine on the spool).

12. WRAP BUNDLE

Working with the tail end of the twine, wrap diagonally up the bundle and back down again so that the two layers crisscross. Secure with a knot in the back.

13. REMOVE RUBBER BAND

Using one blade of a scissor, gently pull the rubber band out and snip to release it. Then, complete the step by pulling the rubber band out from your bundle with your fingers.

14. SNIP LOOSE ENDS

Using sharp scissors (or garden shears if necessary), blunt the end of the greens so that they are even and blunt. Note: You want the greens to extend about 1" beyond the palo santo (and not be even with it).

15. FINISHING TOUCH

Review your bundle from all angles. Clip any unwanted or ill-positioned greens. The cedar is highly textured (i.e., sticks out of the bundle a lot), so you may wish to trim it back a bit.

Peace and Protection Amethyst Smudge

with Sage, Rosemary, Pink Rose & Amethyst

Protect your peace, get rid of toxicity, cleanse your space, cultivate love.

Unknown

Creating boundaries and protection for our hearts and minds is critical to our well-being. But protection can sometimes manifest in an unhealthy way. How do we protect ourselves in ways that support our highest good?

SUGGESTED INTENTION:

As I burn this rosemary protection smudge, may it call in all the protective energies to fully and profoundly support me and keep me from harm.

INGREDIENTS

- Lavender, 21 small sprigs (nonflowering)—serenity, peace, calm
- Rosemary—strength, protection, memory
- Sage, 5 stems—purification
- Rose (dark pink), 1 stem—love, beauty, happiness, blessings
- Corn husk (dried)
- Amethyst—clears negative energy
- Basting twine
- Twine (brown)

Note: This is an intentionally decorative design. Remove crystal and corn husk before burning.

1 ### GATHER YOUR MATERIALS

You will need sage and lavender for your base, pink rose for color, dried corn husk for a decorative wrap, and an amethyst (if desired) for additional protection and a beautiful finishing touch.

2

3

4

5

2. GATHER SAGE

Pick up your first stem of sage and position it on your hand. Layer each additional stem, one on top of the other, so that they form a balanced bundle.

3. ADD MOST OF LAVENDER

One by one, add all but three stems of your lavender to your bundle, on top of the sage. Note: If your lavender is varying sizes, clip stalks to even length before bundling.

4. ADD ROSE

Snip your rose from the stem (spray roses typically have multiple flowers on each stem) and layer it on top of the lavender and center on your bundle.

5. ADD REMAINING LAVENDER

Layer the remaining three stems of lavender to your bundle. The idea is to cover the rose stem in lavender and have some lavender peeking out around the rose base.

6

7

8

9

6. SECURE TWINE WITH KNOT

Wrap one layer of twine around your bundle, flip the bundle, and secure the twine with a knot on the backside. Note: Because the rose head is rather larger, it is best to secure your bundle at the top versus the bottom.

7. WRAP BUNDLE WITH TWINE

Working with the tail of the twine, wrap diagonally down the bundle and back up again so that the two layers crisscross. Secure the two ends of the twine at the top with a knot. Set your bundle aside.

8. CUT HUSK AND BASTE BUNDLE

With your scissors, cut a strip of corn husk about 2.5" wide and the length of the husk. Be sure to cut against the grain. Note: If your husk is too dry and brittle, spray it with warm water to soften it and avoid tearing.

9. WRAP HUSK

Wrap the husk strip around the bundle. Hold the husk in place with your finger.

10

10. ADD AMETHYST

Position the amethyst on the front center of the bundle (still securing the bundle with your hand). Grab your twine and position it on top of the stone.

11. WRAP BUNDLE WITH TWINE

Join the twine on the back of the bundle and secure it with a knot. Continue wrapping the twine around the amethyst to ensure it stays in place. Several wraps will be necessary. Note: The amethyst is decorative and may want to slide. This is okay, since it is removed before burning and not a permanent part of your bundle.

11

12. FINISHING TOUCH

Review your bundle from all angles. Clip any unwanted or ill-positioned petals or leaves. Remember to let your bundle rest in a cool, dry place for four to six weeks before burning (due to the amethyst inclusion, it is not recommended to hang this bundle). Remove the amethyst and corn husk before burning.

12

Romance Smudge

with Sage, Red Rose & Baby's Breath

Your task is not to seek for love, but merely to seek and find all the barriers within yourself that you have built against it.

Rumi

We long for love and connection. Our brains are wired for it. And sometimes it can be a challenge both to find it and to maintain it.

SUGGESTED INTENTION:

As I burn this smudge, I invite vibrant loving energy into my heart and body. I open my heart and mind to letting go of whatever is in me that may be in the way of the love that is my birthright. May I know myself as both loving and loved. And may I love myself.

INGREDIENTS

- Sage, 9 stems—purification
- Baby's breath, 1 stem
- Rose (miniature, 6 flowers)—love, beauty, happiness, blessings
- Twine (white)
- Love letter (copy) or scrapbook paper (optional)
- Tape

1 GATHER YOUR MATERIALS

You will need sage for your base, red rose for color and as a symbol of love, and baby's breath for texture. Also, if desired, a photocopy of a love letter (or scrapbook paper) for a decorative wrap.

2. GATHER SAGE

Pick up your first stem of sage and position it on your hand. Layer each additional stem, one on top of the other, so that they form a balanced bundle.

3. ADD ROSE

Clip a stem of roses from your rose plant (typically there will be multiple blooms on one stem) and layer it on top of the sage, just below the tallest sage leaves (so each ingredient can be seen).

4. LAYER BABY'S BREATH

Snip a small sprig of baby's breath from the stem (about 1" shorter than your rose) and layer it onto your bundle, so it starts just below the rose heads.

5

5. WRAP BUNDLE WITH TWINE

Wrap one layer of twine around the bottom of your bundle and flip it; secure with a knot. Using the long tail of your twine, continue to wrap up the bundle diagonally to the top (just under baby's breath) and then back down again, crisscrossing along the way. Tie both ends at the bottom with another knot to secure your bundle.

6. PREPARE DECORATIVE WRAP

Using a photocopy of an actual love letter, or a piece of scrapbook paper in the style of one, cut your decorative wrap to about 2.5" tall and 6" wide.

6

7. SECURE DECORATIVE WRAP

Securing the bundle in your hand, gently wrap the decorative wrap (or love letter) around your bundle. Secure with tape (or rewrap with twine if desired). Note: Be sure to remove decorative wrap prior to burning.

8. FINISHING TOUCH

Review your bundle from all angles. Clip any unwanted or ill-positioned leaves or petals. Remember to hang your bundle in a cool, dry place for four to six weeks prior to burning.

Good-Vibes Smudge

with Mixed Flowers & Herbs

You will never be able to escape from your heart. So, it's better to listen to what it has to say.

Paulo Coelho

It can be easy to overlook our desires. Our everyday lives demand our attention, and we can get focused on what is right in front of us rather than what is within us. It's so important that we take the time to slow down and turn inward to get a more clear picture of what we most desire in life.

SUGGESTED INTENTION:

As I burn this vibrant smudge, I call upon my deepest desires from the innermost part of me. What is it that I most dearly want to manifest at this time? I invoke all the loving and positive energies available to me, that they may surround me and support me in bringing my dream into reality.

INGREDIENTS

- Sage (6 stalks)—purification
- Baby's breath
- Delphinium
- Dusty miller
- Carnation (light pink, large)—heart healing, love
- Eucalyptus—fresh energy, revival, renewal
- Statice (purple)
- Yarrow—strength
- Goldenrod
- Liatris
- Thistle—protection
- Twine (pink)

1 GATHER YOUR MATERIALS

This is a big bundle with lots of good stuff! You will need sage for the base and delphinium, carnation, statice, and purple flower for color. You will also need baby's breath, yarrow and thistle for texture, and dusty miller for a finishing touch on the backside.

This is an abundant smudge filled with various ingredients. Don't worry if you cannot access the exact flowers that we used. Get creative! Use what you are drawn-to and what is local.

2. GATHER SAGE AND POSITION TWINE

Organize your sage into two neat halves. Turn one half upside down and join it to the other so there are leaves at both ends; this will create a balanced bundle with thickness at top and bottom. It is wise to position your twine underneath your bundle at this time to make wrapping easier later.

3. ADD LARGE PINK CARNATIONS

Position three carnations in a vertical row down the center of your bundle, leaving some room at the top for the sage to peek out. Trim the carnation stems to be blunt with the bottom of the sage.

4. ADD STATICE

Add a stem of statice to each side of the carnations. Adjust positioning to suit your own eye. I have layered one higher on the left and lower on the right. Trim stems to be blunt with bottom of sage.

5. ADD LIATRIS

Position your liatris on the bundle (where you would like; I put mine behind carnation to distribute the color) and snip stem to be blunt with bottom of bundle.

6. ADD GOLDENROD

Turn goldenrod upside down and position it on your bundle. Insert the stem so that it fits just under the carnation heads. This will allow the yellow flower to cover the stems and thus add color and texture to the bottom half of the bundle.

7. ADD DELPHINIUM

Again, turn your flower upside down and insert the stem under the yellow flower, bringing even more color to the bottom half of your bundle.

8. ADD BABY'S BREATH

Snip two short sprigs of baby's breath from the main stem and insert them on either side of your bundle, filling your bundle with texture.

9. ADD EUCALYPTUS

Position eucalyptus stem onto bundle and clip length to be blunt with bottom of the bundle. Add the stem to your bundle. I have chosen to wrap it around the carnation on the right side. Flip the bundle and add dusty miller to the back to give it a finished look.

10. WRAP BUNDLE WITH TWINE

Wrap the twine around the bundle (just below the carnation), and secure it with a knot. Wrap downward diagonally until you reach the bottom of the bundle; then wrap up the bundle, crisscrossing over the first wrap. Remember to hang your bundle in a cool, dry place for four to six weeks before burning.

Purification Smudge

with Palo Santo, Eucalyptus, Rose, Sage Leaf & Selenite

May you be safe, may you be healthy, may you be happy, may you live with ease.

Unknown

Living life can build up negativity in our bodies. It is important to regularly cleanse ourselves of this energy.

SUGGESTED INTENTION:

May this palo santo cleanse me of and protect me from negative energy. May I be surrounded by a barrier that lets in only positive energy. May I feel ease and contentment.

INGREDIENTS (Makes two)

Palo santo, 2 sticks—creativity, purification
Eucalyptus (silver dollar), 1 stem—fresh energy, revival, renewal
Sage,1 leaf—purification
Rose (pink, small), 2 stems—love, beauty, happiness, blessings
Selenite, 2 crystals—cleansing, clarity
Rubber band (optional)
Twine (white, thin)

Note: This is an intentionally minimalist design. It is perfect as an energetic self-care cleanse but can also be used as a bedside display or beautiful gift for a loved one. Remove selenite before burning.

1   GATHER YOUR MATERIALS

You will need palo santo for the base, eucalyptus for texture, rose for color, sage leaf for decorative wrap, and selenite for additional cleansing.

4

2. PLACE EUCALYPTUS

Position the eucalyptus stem on your palo santo, and clip the bottom of the stem so it is blunt with the bottom of the palo santo. Prune individual eucalyptus leaves as necessary to achieve the desired look.

3. ADD ROSE

Trim one individual rose flower from the main stem (spray roses typically grow in clusters, so you will remove just one flower). Position the rose so that it is equal to the length as the palo santo, and trim stem accordingly.

4. POSITION SELENITE

Lay the selenite directly over the rose stem. It may want to roll a bit, but just secure it down with your hand for now.

5. SECURE LAYERS

At this point, you should have a "sandwich" of palo santo, eucalyptus, rose, and selenite as shown. Secure temporarily with a rubber band at this point if you find that the bundle is difficult to keep intact.

6. ADD SAGE LEAF

Trim one sage leaf off the main stem and wrap it around your bundle, creating a decorative warp around your bundle.

7. SECURE WITH TWINE

Wrap twine around the bundle; continue rewrapping around your first layer four more times (or until you feel the bundle is properly secured). Secure ends of twine by tying a knot on the backside. Remove rubber band if one was used prior to secure.

8. FINISHING TOUCH

It is recommended that this bundle be used for gift giving or display immediately (when ingredients are fresh). For burning, disassemble and burn palo santo. Dried sage and eucalyptus leaves can be burned separately in an abalone shell or fireproof bowl.

Peace and Harmony Smudge

with Sweetgrass & Marigold Wand

Hear blessings drop their blossoms around you.

Rumi

What are the things in our lives that make us lose track of time? Doing these things lowers our heart rates, releases "happiness" hormones, and increases our feelings of peace and harmony. Can you set an intention to dedicate time to doing more of those things?

SUGGESTED INTENTION:

As I burn this bright and beautiful smudge, may I breathe in deeply and visualize all that brings me peace and harmony. Like pulling on a silken rope, may I imagine drawing it all to me, hand over hand. And with each pull may I feel my heart fill, my muscles relax, and my sense of contentment rise.

INGREDIENTS

- Sweetgrass, 1 braid (dried)—healing, peace, and positivity
- Marigold, 3 flowers (or potted plant to snip from)—warmth
- Toothpick
- Twine (orange)

1 GATHER YOUR MATERIALS
You will need marigold and a sweetgrass braid.

2

3

4

2. SECURE SWEETGRASS

Fold the sweetgrass braid in half and secure the bottom with twine.

3. SNIP MARIGOLD

Snip three individual marigold flowers and stems from the plant. It is important to leave the stems as long as possible.

4. REMOVE LEAVES

Using your garden scissors, gently remove the leaves from each marigold so that only the flower and stem remain on each one.

5. ARRANGE MARIGOLDS

Review your marigolds and decide what order you will place them on the sweetgrass. I choose to put the largest flower in the center, between two smaller marigolds. Set aside.

6. PIERCE BRAID

Position a toothpick approximately 1.5" from the top of the braid. Piece the toothpick through the opening where the individual strands converge. Press the toothpick gently, but firmly, until it is through both layers.

7. INSERT FIRST MARIGOLD

Hold the marigold by the stem and gently insert it into the hole drilled by the toothpick. Wiggle the toothpick as needed to open the hole as needed. Remove toothpick after stem is fully inserted.

5

6

7

8. REPEAT

Following the instructions in step 7, repeat, inserting two additional marigolds down the length of the sweetgrass.

9. SECURE WITH TWINE

Wrap one layer of the twine around the base of the sweetgrass, approximately 1" from the bottom. Flip the bundle and secure the twine with a knot on the backside (leaving a long tail on the spool).

10. WRAP UPWARD

Working with the tail of the twine, wrap diagonally all the way up the bundle. Be sure to wrap directly across each marigold to tether it to the bundle. Wrap until you have covered the top marigold.

11. WRAP DOWNWARD

After reaching the top, switch directions and begin wrapping diagonally toward the bottom, crisscrossing each strand on the way down. When you reach the bottom, wrap five or more loops around the base of the braid for a finishing touch and then secure twine with a knot in the back.

12. FINISHING TOUCH

Review your bundle from all angles. Make any necessary adjustments, since the marigolds may have shifted during the wrapping process. Your bundle is complete. Allow it to dry for four weeks (or until the marigolds are dry) before burning.

Festive Holiday Smudge
with Cedar, Juniper, Rosemary, and Cinnamon

Gratitude is not only the greatest of virtues, but the parent of all others.

Cicero

As we reach the end of the year and we find ourselves in the season of winter, where heat and light are scarce, may we turn inward, rest, and focus on warming our hearts. Gratitude can stoke the fire in our hearts. Meditating on all the gifts that we have in our lives—perhaps within us, but also within our relationships—adds fuel to our heart's fire. How do we feed our hearts with gratitude to keep ourselves and those we love warm during this cold wintertime? How do we build those fires to take us into a new beginning with peace and purpose?

SUGGESTED INTENTION:

As I burn this aromatic smudge, may I inhale fully and visualize a warm, glowing fire within my heart. May I feel the warmth travel from my heart throughout my body, and may I see myself being filled with warm sustenance. As I visualize all that I am grateful for, may I know myself as blessed. And may I take the warmth in my heart, share it with others, and bring it into the new year.

INGREDIENTS

- Cedar, 5 boughs (approximately 14" long) —releasing negativity, cleansing
- Rosemary, 3 sprigs—strength, protection, memory
- Juniper, 2 stems (approximately 7" long) —protection, prosperity, cleansing
- Cinnamon stick, red rose, baby's breath, anise (optional)
- Twine (red/white)

1 GATHER YOUR MATERIALS

You will need cedar for the base of this bundle and rosemary and juniper for additional aromatic accents. If desired, add cinnamon stick, anise, baby's breath, and red rose petals to increase the festive flair.

2. GATHER CEDAR

Layer your cedar boughs, one on top of the other, alternating orientation as needed (i.e., turning individual branches upside down to fill out both sides evenly).

3. SHAPE CEDAR

Hold the cedar in both hands, as shown. Bend the cedar so that it folds in the middle, doubling it in width and shortening it in length. This may take some strength since the cedar can be quite sturdy.

4. ADD JUNIPER

Where you position the juniper will depend on the size and shape of your clipping. Mine was short and wide, so I decided to add it toward the bottom, where my bundle needed more bulk.

5. ADD ROSEMARY AND BASTE

Holding your bundle firmly in your hand, layer the rosemary on the top over the cedar and juniper. Now is a good time to add any additional holiday ingredients if desired (mentioned in the list provided) and to baste your bundle, since it is likely getting unwieldy.

6. SECURE TWINE

Wrap one layer of twine around the bottom of your bundle, approximately 1" from the bottom. Secure the twine with a knot on the backside (leaving a long tail of twine).

7. WRAP BUNDLE WITH TWINE

Working with the tail, wrap your twine diagonally up the bundle and back down again so that the two layers crisscross. Secure the two ends of twine at the bottom with a knot.

8. FINISHING TOUCHES

With your garden scissors, clip off any unwanted cedar that is poking through the twine; there is likely a lot of it! Snip to your own liking. Then be sure to hang the bundle in a cool, dry location for four to six weeks before burning. Enjoy as you celebrate your winter holiday season!

8

14

Wedding Smudge
with White Sage, Rosemary, Eucalyptus & White Rose

Love must be as much a light, as it is a flame.

Henry David Thoreau

Your partner is your soul's most mirroring shadow—your playmate, your rock, your taker of care, and your partner in crime. As you join your lives and energies together, may you know your lives as bigger, brighter, and fuller. May you feel the love of all who came before you, who in loving you taught you to love. May you rest and rise in the power and beauty of everlasting love.

SUGGESTED INTENTION:

As I burn this powerful smudge, I close my eyes and know myself as deeply held in the warmth of everlasting love. I feel the joy and excitement at this amazing and beautiful experience, and my fears are few. I focus on all the loving energies around me who hope for this love to stay vibrant and strong, both those who are still with me and those that have passed. I feel deep gratitude for all the love that has been given to me in my life, and honor and appreciate those who cannot be with me today.

INGREDIENTS

- Eucalyptus (silver dollar), 1 stem—fresh energy, revival, renewal
- White sage, 1 large bundle (dried)—purification
- Rosemary, 3 stems—strength, protection, memory
- Rose (white), 4 flowers—love, beauty, happiness, blessings
- Lace, white (or another desired wrap)
- Twine
- Ring (optional)
- Lace ribbon (optional)

Note: This is an intentionally decorative design. Remove lace and ring before burning.

1 GATHER YOUR MATERIALS

You will need a prepurchased or predried white sage bundle for your base and primary source of burning, eucalyptus and rosemary for texture, and white roses for a touch of elegance. Additionally, you may wish to add a symbolic ring and lace trimming as shown.

2

3

4

2. PREPARING RING

Cut a piece of twine, approximately 14" long, and fasten it to the back of your ring. Let both tails trail, equally. Insert rosemary stalks into the center of the ring. Add or subtract rosemary so that it is a snug fit within the ring. Set aside.

3. MEASURE EUCALYPTUS

Layer eucalyptus on the sage, and position it so that the top leaf sticks out above the sage. Snip end so it is blunted with sage. Set aside.

4. POSITION ROSEMARY AND RING

Layer the rosemary and ring on top of the sage; let the tails of the twine hang out on either side of the sage.

5

5. POSITION EUCALYPTUS

Bring the precut eucalyptus stem to the back of your sage and position it as planned, with the height of one leaf sticking out above the top of the sage. Hold the entire bundle in your hand and get ready to wrap.

6. SECURE TWINE WITH KNOT

Pull both ends of the twine to the back of the bundle and tie with a knot. Wrap another loop to ensure that it is secure. Set aside.

6

7. TRIM ROSES

Using your garden scissors, trim individual roses off the main stem; this will ensure that they are easier to insert into your bundle.

8. POSITION ROSES

Slide each of the three roses into the center of the ring, positioning them as is pleasing to your eye. I followed the shape of my ring, with two lower on either side and one higher in the middle.

9. TRIM ROSES

If necessary, trim the rose stems so that they are blunt with the bottom of the sage bundle.

10. ADD DECORATIVE LACE

Cut a piece of lace 3" wide by 16" long and wrap it around the base of your bundle, tucking under your ring so as not to obscure it. Tie your lace in the back.

11. FINISHING TOUCHES

Review your bundle from all angles and make any necessary adjustments to suit your style and taste. It is recommended that this bundle be used for gift giving or display immediately (when ingredients are fresh). Remove all decorative elements prior to burning.